W9-BYQ-465

INDIANS OF THE PLAINS AND GREAT BASIN

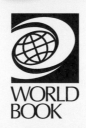

WORLD BOOK

World Book
a Scott Fetzer company
Chicago
www.worldbookonline.com

World Book, Inc.
233 N. Michigan Avenue
Chicago, IL 60601
U.S.A.

For information about other World Book publications, visit our
Web site at http://www.worldbookonline.com or call
1-800-WORLDBK (967-5325).
For information about sales to schools and libraries, call
1-800-975-3250 (United States), or 1-800-837-5365 (Canada).

Library of Congress Cataloging-in-Publication Data

Indians of the Plains and Great Basin.
    p. cm.--(Early peoples)
  Includes index.
  Summary: "A discussion of the Indians of the Plains, including who
the people were, where they lived, the rise of civilization, social structure,
religion, art and architecture, science and technology, daily life,
entertainment and sports, and fall of civilization. Features include
timelines, fact boxes, glossary, list of recommended readings and web sites,
and index"--Provided by publisher.
  ISBN 978-0-7166-2139-3
  1. Indians of North America--Great Plains--History--Juvenile literature.
2. Indians of North America--Great Plains--Social life and customs--
Juvenile literature. 3. Indians of North America--Great Basin--History--
Juvenile literature. 4. Indians of North America--Great Basin--Social life
and customs--Juvenile literature. I. World Book, Inc.
E78.G73I547 2009
978.004'97--dc22
                        2008039344

Printed in China by Leo Paper Products Ltd.,
Heshan, Guangdong
2nd printing June 2010

STAFF

EXECUTIVE COMMITTEE
President
  Paul A. Gazzolo
Vice President and Chief Marketing Officer
  Patricia Ginnis
Vice President and Chief Financial Officer
  Donald D. Keller
Vice President and Editor in Chief
  Paul A. Kobasa
Director, Human Resources
  Bev Ecker
Chief Technology Officer
  Tim Hardy
Managing Director, International
  Benjamin Hinton

EDITORIAL
Editor in Chief
  Paul A. Kobasa
Associate Director, Supplementary
Publications
  Scott Thomas
Managing Editor, Supplementary
Publications
  Barbara A. Mayes
Senior Editor, Supplementary Publications
  Kristina Vaicikonis
Manager, Research, Supplementary
Publications
  Cheryl Graham
Manager, Contracts and Compliance
  (Rights & Permissions)
  Loranne K. Shields

Administrative Assistant
  Ethel Matthews
Editors
  Nicholas Kilzer
  Scott Richardson
  Christine Sullivan

GRAPHICS AND DESIGN
Associate Director
  Sandra M. Dyrlund
Manager
  Tom Evans
Coordinator, Design Development and
Production
  Brenda B. Tropinski

EDITORIAL ADMINISTRATION
Director, Systems and Projects
  Tony Tills
Senior Manager, Publishing Operations
  Timothy Falk

PRODUCTION
Director, Manufacturing and Pre-Press
  Carma Fazio
Manufacturing Manager
  Steve Hueppchen
Production/Technology Manager
  Anne Fritzinger
Production Specialist
  Curley Hunter
Proofreader
  Emilie Schrage

MARKETING
Chief Marketing Officer
  Patricia Ginnis
Associate Director, School and Library
Marketing
  Jennifer Parello

Produced for World Book by
White-Thomson Publishing Ltd.
+44 (0)845 362 8240
www.wtpub.co.uk
Steve White-Thomson, President

Writer: Stephanie Fitzgerald
Editors: Kelly Davis, Robert Famighetti
Designer: Clare Nicholas
Photo Researcher: Amy Sparks
Map Artist: Stefan Chabluk
Illustrator: Adam Hook (p. 21)
Fact Checker: Chelsey Hankins
Proofreader: Kelly Davis
Indexer: Nila Glikin

Consultant:
Akim Reinhardt
Associate Professor of History
Towson University, Towson, Maryland

TABLE OF CONTENTS

Glossary There is a glossary on pages 60-61. Terms defined in the glossary are in type **that looks like this** on their first appearance on any spread (two facing pages).

Additional Resources Books for further reading and recommended Web sites are listed on page 62. Because of the nature of the Internet, some Web site addresses may have changed since publication. The publisher has no responsibility for any such changes or for the content of cited sources.

WHO WERE THE INDIANS OF THE PLAINS AND GREAT BASIN?

American Indian groups have lived in North America for thousands of years. Although experts know little about the earliest groups, **archaeologists** have pieced together some of their story by studying the remains of the people and their **culture**. Such **artifacts** as pottery, stone tools, bones of human beings and animals, and charcoal from campfires have offered clues about how and when the early Indians lived. But many questions remain unanswered.

The first known human inhabitants of North America are known as **Paleo-Indians**. Archaeologists believe they probably arrived around 13,500 years ago. Evidence suggests that people have been living in the Plains and Great Basin areas for more than 12,000 years. Although their lifestyles were quite different, they did share the challenge of survival in these harsh territories.

Life on the Plains

The people who lived on the plains comprised more than 30 different groups. Each had its own distinct language, culture, and system of beliefs. Yet experts often divide the various **tribes** into two groups.

The so-called farming and hunting peoples lived on the prairies. These people lived in villages for most of the year, where they raised such crops as corn, beans, and squash. They also hunted small

◀ A member of the Shoshone tribe, Summer Baldwin, in traditional dress, stands before the Sacagawea *(sah kah guh WEE uh)* Peaks in Idaho. The mountains were named for her ancestor, Sacagawea, who accompanied Lewis and Clark on their famous 1804–1806 expedition through what is now the Northwest (see page 54).

▲ Before the arrival of Europeans, prairie grasses covered large portions of the plains. Few trees grew in the region, except along rivers and creeks.

game and gathered wild foods near their villages. Twice a year, these tribes would venture farther away from home to participate in large bison *(BY suhn)* hunts.

The other groups of Plains Indians were the **nomadic** tribes that moved from place to place, hunting bison. Among these were the Arapaho, Crow, Blackfeet (also known in some places as Blackfoot), and Sioux. All were well known for their elaborate war bonnets and beautifully decorated **tipis** (also spelled tepees).

Basin Dwellers

The people of the Great Basin area were extremely resourceful. Such tribes as the Shoshone, Paiute, and Ute lived in an area of North America that is made up largely of mountains, canyons, and deserts. The climate is harsh, and the area did not provide the people of the Great Basin with much wild food. The land was not suitable for farming, and there were few game animals for hunting. Nevertheless, the Indians of the Great Basin managed to carve out a successful way of life in this demanding environment for thousands of years.

TRIBES OF THE PLAINS AND GREAT BASIN

Some of these tribe names are very common today, but many of them were actually given by Europeans.

Farmer-Hunter Tribes of the Prairies
Arikara *(uh RIHK uh ruh)*
Hidatsa *(hih DAHT sah)*
Iowa *(EYE uh wuh)*
Kansa *(KAN saw)*
Mandan *(MAN dan)*
Missouri *(muh ZUR ee)*
Omaha *(OH muh haw)*
Osage *(OH sayj)*
Oto *(OHT oh)*
Pawnee *(paw NEE)*
Ponca *(PAHN kuh)*
Quapaw *(KWAH paw)*
Wichita *(WHICH uh taw)*

Nomadic Hunting Tribes of the Great Plains
Arapaho *(uh RAP uh hoh)*
Assiniboine *(uh SIHN uh boyn)*
Blackfeet (also known in some
    regions as Blackfoot)
Cheyenne *(shy EHN)*
Comanche *(kuh MAN chee)*
Crow
Gros Ventre *(groh VAHNT)*
Kiowa *(KY uh wuh)*
Kitsai *(kiht SY)*
Plains Apache *(uh PACH ee)*
Plains Cree
Plains Ojibwa *(oh JIHB way)*
Sioux *(soo)* (also known as Dakota *[duh KOH tuh]*,
    Lakota *[luh KOH tuh]*, or Nakota *[nuh KOH tuh]*)
Tonkawa *(TONG kuh wah)*

Tribes of the Great Basin
Bannock *(BAN uhk)*
Paiute *(py YOOT)*
Shoshone *(shoh SHOH nee)*
Ute *(yoot)*

WHERE DID THE INDIANS OF THE PLAINS AND GREAT BASIN LIVE?

Taken together, the Plains and Great Basin regions cover a huge part of North America. Many different habitats can be found inside this large territory.

A Sea of Grass

The North American Plains region is a vast grassland, covering some 3.2 million square miles (8.3 million square kilometers) in what is now the United States and Canada.

The region includes parts of the present-day states of Arkansas, Colorado, Iowa, Kansas, Minnesota, Missouri, Montana, Nebraska, New Mexico, North Dakota, Oklahoma, South Dakota, Texas, and Wyoming. It extends north to include parts of the Canadian provinces of Alberta, Manitoba, and Saskatchewan.

The North American Plains consist of two kinds of grasslands. The eastern area, near the Mississippi Valley, receives plentiful rainfall. The region is often referred to as the tall grass plains or the prairie. It is suitable for farming and was home to the farmer-hunter **tribes.** Less rain falls in the western part of the plains, which was covered by short grasses. The area is known as the High Plains, the Great Plains, or simply the Plains. The **nomadic** hunting tribes—and their favorite prey, the bison— flourished in this region.

▼ Regions of the Plains inhabited by various Indian tribes in 1800, before their way of life was changed by the arrival of large numbers of people of European descent.

Plains

CANADA

PLAINS CREE
BLACKFOOT
PLAINS OJIBWA
ASSINIBOINE
GROS VENTRE
Missouri River
HIDATSA
CROW
SIOUX
MANDAN
ARIKARA
SIOUX
SIOUX
CHEYENNE
SIOUX
PONCA
OMAHA
PAWNEE
IOWA
OTO
ARAPAHO
MISSOURI
KANSA
KIOWA
OSAGE
QUAPAW
PLAINS APACHE
UNITED STATES
COMANCHE
WICHITA
KITSAI
MEXICO
TONKAWA

Canada
United States
Mexico

Mississippi River
Rio Grande

500 Miles
500 Kilometers

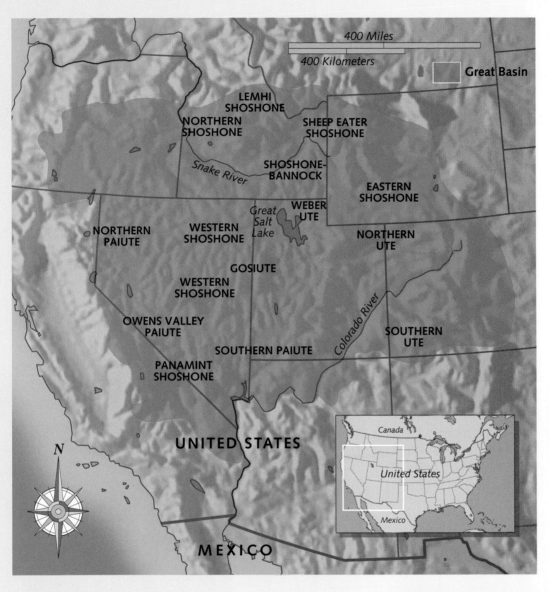

400 Miles
400 Kilometers

Great Basin

LEMHI
SHOSHONE
NORTHERN
SHOSHONE
SHEEP EATER
SHOSHONE
Snake River
SHOSHONE-
BANNOCK
EASTERN
SHOSHONE
WEBER
UTE
*Great
Salt
Lake*
NORTHERN
PAIUTE
WESTERN
SHOSHONE
NORTHERN
UTE
GOSIUTE
WESTERN
SHOSHONE
Colorado River
OWENS VALLEY
PAIUTE
SOUTHERN
UTE
SOUTHERN PAIUTE
PANAMINT
SHOSHONE
UNITED STATES

N

MEXICO

Canada

United States

Mexico

◀ Areas where major tribes of the Great Basin lived in 1800. Scholars used language to group the Basin Indians into tribes. The tribes of the Great Basin were further divided into smaller groups based on similar dialects, **cultures,** and history.

A Harsh Landscape

The Great Basin covers about 200,000 square miles (520,000 square kilometers) of some of the harshest land in North America. The Basin includes all of the present-day states of Nevada and Utah and parts of Arizona, California, Colorado, Idaho, Montana, New Mexico, Oregon, and Wyoming.

The Basin is the driest spot in North America, but it does contain some plant life, as well as small lakes, rivers, and creeks. Without these water sources, of course, human beings could never live in the region. Even so, the search for good water sources played a significant part in the lives of the Indians of the Great Basin.

PLAINS AND BASIN ANIMALS

The Plains were home to many kinds of animals, most famously the bison (also known as the American buffalo). Such other grazing animals as deer, elk, and antelope also shared these grasslands. Bears, coyotes, prairie dogs, rabbits, and wolves were common. Antelope and bison could also be found in the Basin. But such smaller animals as gophers, rabbits, and squirrels were more common.

THE FIRST INDIANS

Archaeologists working in the Plains region have discovered the remains of mammoths that had been hunted, killed, and eaten by human beings. They have also found such **artifacts** as stone tools and **ornaments** made of antler and bone. These finds led experts to conclude that Indians lived in the area more than 11,000 years ago.

Mummy Cave in Wyoming was used by at least 30 groups of Indians for thousands of years. Artifacts found there range from about 400 to 10,000 years old. Because of the area's dry climate, **perishable** items—cords, nets, feathers, and moccasins—

SPIRIT CAVE MAN

One way archaeologists can learn about ancient peoples is by studying their remains. However, many modern American Indians see this practice as disrespectful and oppose the study and display of their ancestors' skeletons. The Native American Graves Protection and Repatriation Act (NAGPRA) of 1990 provides a process by which remains can be returned to their rightful owners. Although NAGPRA resulted in the repatriation (return) of many remains and ceremonial items, proving ownership can sometimes be difficult. Spirit Cave Man, a partially mummified skeleton discovered in a Nevada cave on government land, became the center of a dispute between the Fallon-Shoshone Paiute Tribe and the U.S. Bureau of Land Management. The tribe sought to take possession of the 9,400-year-old remains for reburial under NAGPRA. However, Bureau scientists in 2000 determined that the tribe could not prove a direct relationship to Spirit Cave Man, and therefore the remains would not be turned over. The remains are currently in storage at the Nevada State Museum in Carson City, and the tribe is continuing its efforts to take possession of them.

▼ The archaeological site at Hell Gap, Wyoming, contains evidence of habitation from more than 12,000 years ago. It includes the remains of dwellings, stone and bone tools, stone and bone ornaments, and animal bones. Among other things, this site gave experts new insight into the hunting techniques of the Indians who lived in the area.

were preserved. The cave was named for a perfectly preserved 700-year-old mummy found there.

In the Beginning

The first people who lived in the Plains and Great Basin areas are referred to as **Paleo-Indians**. These early Indians hunted such **megafauna** as mammoths, giant bison, and mastodons. About 8,000 years ago, the megafauna began to disappear. Many scientists believe that a drastic change in climate might have caused their decline.

During this time, known as the Archaic Period, many people **migrated** out of the Plains area. Those who stayed changed the way they lived. They were still **nomadic** hunters, but they focused more on smaller game and gathering wild foods.

On the eastern edge of the plains, another radical change occurred. During what is called the Plains

▲ Archaeologists believe that Danger Cave, a large limestone cavern in the Bonneville Basin of western Utah, provides evidence that people lived there some 9,000 years ago. In the cave, scientists have found baskets, wood and bone tools, weapons, and pieces of nets used for catching animals.

Woodland period, Indians began to live in semipermanent villages. They practiced farming on a small scale and built mounds to bury their dead. Eventually these groups relied more on farming, ushering in the period known as Plains Village. During the Plains Woodland and Village periods, the farming influence spread farther and farther west. However, there were always **tribes** that continued with a nomadic hunting and gathering way of life.

Early inhabitants of the Great Basin also lived in different ways. Those who lived near streams practiced farming. Others continued to follow a more nomadic hunting and gathering lifestyle.

Ways of Communicating

Smoke Signal, a statue in Pioneer Park in Lincoln, Nebraska, was erected in the 1930's as a memorial to local tribes. The sculpture shows how Plains Indians communicated over long distances by using fire and a blanket to create smoke signals.

People of European descent settled the Plains and Great Basin relatively late compared with eastern North America. This enabled the Plains and Basin Indians to maintain a traditional way of life longer than many other Indian groups.

The Indians of the Plains and Great Basin did not have much early contact with Europeans. They did, however, gain access to horses brought to the New World by Europeans. Indians in the Southwest obtained horses from the Spanish in the early 1500's. By the 1600's, Plains Indians had horses through trade with their neighbors.

This important development in history enabled Indians to travel great distances with ease. This new freedom of movement brought many different **tribes** into contact with one another. Since each tribe spoke a different language, they had to find a way to communicate.

Talk of the Tribes

Indians developed a sign language that enabled them to communicate with anyone, including Europeans. The word "bison," for example, was indicated by placing bent index fingers on either side of one's head to look like horns. This silent way of "talking" was also used on a hunt or in a war party to communicate without giving away one's position.

▶ *The Blanket Signal,* a painting by American artist Frederic Remington, depicts a mounted Indian using a blanket as a signal. Perhaps he has spotted bison or discovered enemy warriors nearby. Frederic Remington (1861–1909) is known for his depictions of life in the West in the late 1800's.

When they were too far apart to use hand signals, Plains Indians used smoke signals. To send smoke signals, a person built a fire on high ground. He used materials that would burn slowly and create a great deal of smoke, such as damp grass. The signaler would fling a blanket over the fire, and then remove it long enough to release a puff of smoke. Members of the tribe "read" the message based on the number of puffs that had been released.

The discovery signal was another means of communication Indians used. An Indian on horseback first rode around in a circle to attract attention. If the rider held an open blanket over his head and then brought it down toward the ground, it signaled that he had located bison. To show that he had seen enemies, the Indian rode back and forth. He might also wave a blanket over his head or throw it into the air several times. Once the danger passed, the Indian waved an open blanket back and forth in front of his body.

NAME SIGNS

Each tribe had a sign for other tribes. For example, wiping one's hand down the outside of one's right foot, from front to back, as if brushing off dirt, indicated the Blackfeet tribe. Many tribes referred to the Sioux as "cutthroats." The sign for that tribe was a flattened hand, palm down, passed across the throat from left to right.

SOCIAL ORGANIZATION

People usually associate an individual Indian with the **tribe** to which he or she belongs. It was more common, however, for Indians to identify themselves with smaller groups such as **bands** or villages. In fact, whole tribes gathered together only at certain times of the year.

▲ *Indian Women Moving Camp*, a watercolor painting by American artist Charles Marion (1864–1926), depicts a band of Plains Indians on the move. The horses drag palletlike devices called **travois** *(truh VOY)*, which Indians used to transport loads.

People of the Plains

The **nomadic** hunting groups of the Plains tribes were mostly divided into bands. A band was made up of a group of families that traveled, lived, and hunted together. Similarly, the prairie groups were divided into small villages shared by extended family groups.

Many people also identified themselves by their **clan** affiliation. Members of a clan share a common ancestor. Because hundreds or even thousands of people could belong to the same clan, members did not all live in the same village or band. All members of the same clan were considered related, however, no matter where they lived—even if they lived with a different tribe.

For some tribes, such as the Wichita and Mandan, clan membership was traced through the mother. In this **matrilineal** system, a child belonged to the clan of his or her mother. Among other tribes, such as the Omaha, clans were **patrilineal**— membership was through the father.

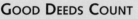
GOOD DEEDS COUNT

In general, having lots of possessions was not important among peoples of the Great Plains. People were respected for their deeds—bravery in war or skill in hunting, for example. When the people began acquiring horses, however, the animals became great status symbols. Again, this had more to do with a person's deeds. A man who owned many horses was able to help those members of the tribe who did not. He might loan a family horses to help them move their belongings or travel to a new hunting ground, for example. Generosity—much more than wealth—was greatly respected among the people of the plains.

▼ A photograph of a band of Paiutes near Cedar, Utah, taken in the early 1870's, shows men dressed in mostly nontraditional clothing. They continued, however, to wear their hair long and, in some cases, braided.

During the summer, various bands would come together as a tribe at a meeting place that had been selected the year before. They would participate in **communal** (group) bison hunts and hold religious ceremonies. This was also a time when important decisions affecting the entire tribe might be made.

People of the Basin

People who lived in the Great Basin were more spread out than those who lived on the Plains. Food and water were scarce in this region, and the land could not support too many people in one area. For most of the year, a small band of families traveled together as they roamed the countryside gathering food. In the winter, only one or two families could live together in the same place.

Basin families, like bands on the Plains, joined together at certain times of the year. Annual antelope and rabbit hunts were a time for many families to gather. Every year, the Paiute came together to harvest piñon *(PIHN yuhn)* nuts. In both cases, these gatherings were a good time for single people to find mates. They were also occasions to hold religious ceremonies. During the piñon harvest, the Northern Paiute started the day with sunrise prayers. There were also nighttime dances held around a fire to give thanks for the harvest and pray for rain.

LEADING THE PEOPLE

The Indians of the Plains and Great Basin had many levels of leadership. In each case, however, leaders were highly respected men who were elected to their positions.

Plains Chiefs

From the family, to the **band**, to the **tribe**, every unit of Plains Indians had a leader or leaders. In a single family, an older man—either a grandfather or father—was the authority. The heads of the families then voted for a man or men to lead the band or village. When the tribe gathered together, the various band or village headmen formed a council.

There were two kinds of headmen, or chiefs, in Plains society—civil leaders and war leaders. Both kinds were chosen based on their experience and character. A civil leader might be an older man who no longer hunted or made war. In fact, he might never have been a warrior. Bravery and hunting skill were highly respected, but so were such traits as generosity and sound judgment. A war leader was more likely to be a younger man who showed great bravery and fighting skills.

▼ Quanah (*KWAH nuh*) Parker was the last chief of the Comanche Indians. He refused to accept the provisions of the 1867 Treaty of Medicine Lodge, which dictated the removal of all southern Plains Indians to a **reservation.** He left the warpath and led his tribe to the reservation only when he realized there was no other choice.

◀ A photo taken in the 1870's of Little Wolf (left), a famous Cheyenne chief and warrior. He stands next to Dull Knife, another Cheyenne chief. After Little Wolf and his band were relocated from Montana to a reservation in Oklahoma in 1876, members of the band began to sicken and die. Little Wolf asked to leave in peace, but his request was denied. In 1878, he successfully led 300 people on the long trek home, eluding the U.S. Army's many attempts to track him down. He and his people remained in Montana.

Civil chiefs guided decision-making for the band, village, or tribe. They offered advice on such matters as when to schedule a hunt and when and where to move the camp. They did not, however, control the group. All of the adult men in the group made decisions jointly, based on the advice of the chiefs.

A war chief, on the other hand, had almost complete control over his war party. He made every important decision, including how and when to fight, where to camp, and when to turn back. He was even in charge of making peace with the enemy. However, the war chief held almost no power during times of peace.

Basin Talkers

Basin groups did not usually have recognized leaders but rather, unofficial leaders, sometimes known as "talkers." A talker was a respected member of the band, to whom others would go for advice.

After certain Basin groups, such as the Ute, obtained horses, a more formal system of leadership evolved. With horses, the Ute were able to join together in larger groups for bison hunts. A chief was needed to organize the hunt.

POLICING THE HUNT

The annual bison hunt was the only peacetime activity during which a war chief or a tribal military society had authority over the entire group. Anyone who jeopardized the hunt—by scaring the herd away or not contributing enough to the effort, for example—would be punished. His possessions might be destroyed, or he might be beaten. In some tribes, such a person could even be killed. This was the only time that the people's behavior was controlled or punished by force.

SPIRITUAL LEADERS

The spirit world was an important part of everyday life for the Indians of the Plains and Great Basin. In fact, they felt it was crucial to their survival. In each region, a religious leader, a **medicine man** or shaman *(SHAH muhn)*, provided the link between the people and the world of spirits. Medicine refers to a powerful, protective spirit; a medicine man thus possessed great medicine.

In Touch with the Spirits

Almost every activity on the Plains and Great Basin involved either offering thanks to or asking for help from the spirit world. A holy person, who could be either a man or an older woman, was the person that spoke to the spirits on behalf of the people. Indians believed that the spirits spoke to people through dreams or visions. A vision was brought on when a person placed physical stress on his or her body. He or she might go for days without food, stay outside in the bitter cold or burning heat, or even cause himself or herself bodily harm. Medicine people were usually particularly good at experiencing visions and dreams, which showed their close contact with the spirit world.

▶ Short Bull (1845–1915), a Sioux medicine man. With Kicking Bear, Short Bull led the Ghost Dance religious movement among the Sioux in 1889 and 1890. Participants believed that the movement would restore their way of life, which had changed with the arrival of Europeans. The movement ended with the massacre at Wounded Knee in December 1890.

THE GREAT SPIRIT

Indians on the Plains and Great Basin believed in a spiritual force that guided every aspect of their lives. Although many ceremonies and rituals had very specific themes, such as ensuring a successful hunt or becoming an adult in a coming-of-age ceremony, all were ultimately directed to this guiding force. The Basin tribes called this spirit Puha *(POO hah)*. The Blackfeet called this great spirit Napi *(NAH pee)*, which means the old man. Among the Sioux and Assiniboine, it was Wakan Tanka *(WAH kahn THAHN kah)*, and the Pawnee called it Tirawa *(tih RAH wah)*.

Other people of the group would consult a medicine man to help explain their own dreams and visions. They would also seek help from the medicine man before such important events as a hunt or raid. Religious leaders also led the **rituals** that were meant to give thanks to the spirit world.

Medicine men held a leadership position among the Plains and Great Basin Indians and had a great deal of influence within the **tribes**. In fact, one of the most famous Indian leaders in history, Sitting Bull, was a medicine man.

A Healing Spirit

Among many tribes, holy men and women were also healers. Among some groups, however, including the Lakota Sioux, priest and healer were separate roles performed by different people. One part of a healer's job was to ask the spirit world for help in healing sickness. Healers also used natural remedies, such as herbs and other plants, to cure illnesses.

▶ Bone figurines, made around A.D. 500, found in Hogup Cave, Utah. Experts believe Basin Indian healers used the figurines in purification rituals.

INDIAN WARRIORS

Warfare was very much a part of the Plains Indians' lives. Honor was gained through a successful raid on another group. Successful warriors were greatly revered.

Making War

Plains Indians fought each other for many reasons. Some fights were merely to gain honor or horses. Sometimes wars were fought over territory or to avenge an earlier attack.

After European settlers began to **encroach** *(ehn KROHCH)* upon their land, the Plains Indians fought for their survival. They defended themselves against settlers who wanted to build houses and plow fields on Indian lands. Later, they fought the United States Army, which was sent to push them off their lands and onto **reservations**, areas of land set aside by a country's government for a special purpose, such as the settlement of Indian tribes.

The Plains Indians engaged in small, quick raids against other **tribes.** However, killing one's enemy was not the best way to show bravery. A warrior sought honor in battle by stealing his enemies' horses or, better yet, by counting coup *(koo)*. The object of counting coup was for a warrior to touch his enemy during the battle. He might touch him with his bow, a **coup stick**, or—best of all—his bare hand. If, after touching his enemy, the warrior managed to kill him, he received even greater honor.

Indians of the Great Basin were mostly peaceful people. They spent much of their time in search of food, leaving

▶ A coup stick used by a Blackfeet warrior. To touch one's enemy with a coup stick during battle was considered an act of great bravery.

▶ A Sioux warrior's shield. Shields were made of rawhide and decorated with painted symbols. The bison was probably a guiding spirit for the warrior who carried this shield.

little time for planning or carrying out raids. As the Indians of the Basin had few possessions, they were not likely targets for other groups. The Northern Paiute, however, did clash with their neighbors from the plains—the Blackfeet and Crow.

Weapons of War

Indians traditionally fought with bows and arrows, clubs, tomahawks, and knives. They protected themselves with shields made from animal hides and decorated with feathers and medicine signs. Medicine, the spirit that protected a warrior in battle, was just as important as any weapon. Warriors sometimes wore breast plates fashioned from bison and bird bones, mainly as decorative or medicine items. They also wore small leather pouches, called medicine bundles. These held **sacred** objects that were supposed to protect the wearer. The medicine signs that a warrior painted on his shield were also meant to protect him from harm. These signs often depicted images that had come to a warrior in his dreams or during the **vision quest ritual**.

A SOLDIER'S UNIFORM

Some warriors went shirtless into battle. They wore only medicine signs painted on their skin for protection. Others wore elaborately decorated shirts made of animal skins. These war shirts might be decorated with beads or porcupine quills that represented awards for past deeds—in much the same way as military medals today. Others might be decorated with painted battle scenes or even the hair of a warrior's enemy.

MEN'S AND WOMEN'S ROLES

Men and women both contributed to the smooth running of an Indian camp. In the Great Basin and on the Plains, each **gender** had a specific set of tasks to perform.

Men at Work

The main responsibilities of Plains Indian men were to hunt, make war, and protect their **band** or village. The tasks that went along with these responsibilities, such as making weapons and teaching young men how to hunt and fight, were also performed by men.

Among the Plains Indians, the leaders were always men. When not hunting or raiding, they met in councils to discuss such tribal affairs as upcoming hunts, raids, or ceremonies. After the Plains Indians obtained horses, the men were in charge of training and caring for their animals.

Men of the Great Basin hunted larger game and made weapons. However, they also gathered some wild foods and collected water and firewood—tasks that on the Plains fell to women.

CRAFTING LEATHER

Plains women were experts at transforming animal hides into leather. First, the woman spread out the hide and pinned it to the ground using wooden stakes. Next, she used a scraper to clean one side of the hide. Sometimes the animal's hair was left on. Alternatively, the woman turned the hide over and scraped off the hair. If she was making rawhide to be used for containers or thongs, the woman allowed the hide to dry into a tough piece of leather. For softer leather for clothing and other household items, the woman rubbed a mixture of brains and fat into the hide and then rubbed and stretched it with a smooth stone or bone.

▶ *The Buffalo Hunt*, a pen and ink drawing by Frederic Remington. Hunting bison on horseback was easier than on foot, but still very dangerous. A fully grown bison can be 6.6 feet (2 meters) in height and weigh as much as 3,900 pounds (1,000 kilograms). The hunters had to get close enough to kill them with spears or bows and arrows.

Women's Work

Plains women accompanied men on big hunting trips so that they could help butcher the game and transport the meat and skins back to their camp or village. Otherwise, they were in charge of the home and the fields. Women took care of the children, gathered water and firewood, and made the everyday items the family used to survive, including clothes, **tipi** covers and furnishings, cooking utensils, baskets, and other containers. They also gathered, stored, and prepared all the wild foods that the family ate, and prepared, cooked, and/or stored the meat provided by the men.

Women on the prairies also planted, tended, and harvested crops. When it was time for a **nomadic** group to move, the women packed up the tipis and household goods, transported them to the new campsite, and set up camp again.

Basin women gathered, prepared, and stored wild food and also hunted small animals. Like the Plains women, they made household items and cared for the children.

▲ An artist's rendering of a Plains Indian village. The roles of men and women were well defined among the Plains **tribes.** Men protected the village, made weapons, and provided meat. Women cared for children, raised crops, gathered wild foods, and prepared the food. They also wove cloth and baskets and cured hides into leather.

CRIME AND PUNISHMENT

There were no written laws among the Plains Indians, but there were very specific understandings of proper behavior. Although Indian **cultures** did not have a police force, there were specific punishments connected with certain crimes. Social behavior was dictated by established customs and, more importantly, by public opinion. Acceptable behavior was encouraged—and unacceptable behavior discouraged—in a variety of ways.

Doing What Is Right

Each society had its own ideas of how individuals should behave. Among the Lakota and Nakota, for example, people were expected to be brave, honest, and generous. It was up to the individual to make sure he or she behaved properly. People were taught what was expected of them from the time they were children. Improper behavior—in a child or an adult—was discouraged or corrected, in many cases, by public humiliation.

People whose actions were considered unacceptable would be **taunted** by the rest of the **tribe**. Sometimes the shame would be so great that the offender would leave the camp to live in **exile**. Living alone on the plains was dangerous. It was difficult for

▼ For Indians on the Plains or in the Great Basin, exile from the tribe was in essence a death sentence. Survival required the efforts of a group—to hunt, gather, and prepare food and to find shelter. A lone person could not defend himself or herself against enemies or predators.

▲ Crow women on horseback, in a photograph from around 1890. Among the Crow Indians, joking with or poking fun at relatives was a way of encouraging good behavior.

JOKING RELATIVES

Among the Crow, there were certain family members who were responsible for controlling social behavior. These "joking relatives" might be cousins or sisters- or brothers-in-law who teased other family members about such things as laziness or a lack of skills. This teasing was meant to encourage the person to behave as a Plains Indian should.

a single person to find and prepare food and other necessities to survive. It was also nearly impossible for a solitary Indian to protect himself or herself against outside threats. For most people, the threat of public shame was enough to ensure proper behavior.

Serious Crimes

There were some crimes so great that more than public humiliation was required to set things right. Behavior that was celebrated in warfare—such as stealing a horse or killing another person—was considered a serious crime when committed against a member of one's own tribe and could result in exile. If a Cheyenne Indian killed another member of the tribe, he or she was sent into exile for 10 years. The murderer's **band** was also forced to move from the camp where the crime had been committed.

Among the Crow and Lakota, murder was considered a private matter. In many cases, the accused murderer was encouraged to provide food or shelter or make other forms of **reparations** *(rehp uh RAY shuhnz)* to the victim's family.

SACRED OBJECTS

acred objects played a large role in the spiritual lives of the Plains and Basin Indians. Some were used in special ceremonies; others were thought to have magical properties that offered protection to the owner.

Sacred Pipes

The sacred pipe, also called the **calumet** *(KAL yuh meht)*, was important in the spiritual lives of both the Plains and Basin Indians. These pipes had long wooden stems and stone bowls, and they were often decorated with quills, feathers, horsehair, and animal fur. (After the Indians began trading with Europeans, they also began decorating their pipes with beads.)

These pipes are often called "peace pipes" because they were smoked at peace councils. For the Indians, the act of smoking a sacred pipe was like a prayer. Sacred pipes were smoked at many ceremonies aside from peace councils.

▼ A medicine bundle with attached weasel skins that belonged to the weasel chapter of the Crow Tobacco Society. During ceremonies, women opened the bundle and danced with the weasel skins to pray for the success of the tobacco crops. Tobacco was grown by the Crow to be used in sacred **rituals.**

Some pipes were reserved for special purposes. Certain Plains **tribes**, including the Pawnee and Omaha, used a special calumet during adoption ceremonies. When a man presented a calumet to a boy or another man, that person became the man's son. Some groups even adopted entire groups of people to form an **alliance**.

Medicine Bundles

Pipes were often kept in medicine bundles, along with other ceremonial objects. Large medicine bundles were often made of whole animal skins that were wrapped around the objects. A holy man kept the medicine bundle for an entire tribe, but individuals could also

The Medicine Wheel

The circle was—and still is—a sacred symbol for the Plains Indians. It represents the cycle of life and the connectedness of all living things. When spokes, or lines, are added inside a circle, it forms a medicine wheel.

Archaeologists have found evidence of many medicine wheels throughout the Great Plains region. The most famous is Bighorn Medicine Wheel in Wyoming, which was constructed by laying stones in a pattern on the ground. No one knows for sure how these wheels were used. Archaeologists have suggested that they might have been used to keep track of the seasons or for important ceremonies.

▲ The Bighorn Medicine Wheel is located atop a 9,642-foot (2,934-meter) mountain in Wyoming. The spot is accessible for only two months of the year—July and August. It is covered in snow the rest of the year. The wheel is 80 feet (24 meters) in diameter and contains 28 spokes radiating out from a cairn (pile of rocks), which forms the hub of the wheel.

have their own bundles. The objects inside were believed to have magical powers. Each object (such as a unique stone or part of an animal) had a special meaning for its owner.

Holy Water

For Indians living in the **arid** Great Basin, water was sacred. They believed that water could purify a person and cure sickness. Some Basin groups believed that if a spell had been cast against a person, he or she could get rid of the evil spirits by taking a bath. Some Indians of the region also believed that tiny spirits, called water babies, lived in the few bodies of water in the area that never went dry.

SACRED CEREMONIES

Indians of the Plains and Great Basin had many ceremonies and **rituals** to keep the spirits happy and to ask for help when it was needed. Experts believe most groups shared two main rituals.

The Sun Dance

Many Plains and Great Basin **tribes** performed a ceremony commonly called a Sun Dance. The Cheyenne called the ceremony the New Life Lodge. The Ponca called it the Mystery Dance. Although there were different names for the ceremony, its purpose was always the same. Men who took part in the ritual were asking the spirit world for an abundance of food, victory over enemies, the healing of the sick, and the general prosperity of the tribe.

The annual Sun Dance was held in summer, when tribes gathered together for the **communal** bison hunt. Particular elements of each tribe's Sun Dance might differ, but one part of the ritual was performed in most versions. Toward the end of the ritual, some men had wooden hooks or skewers driven through the skin of their chests. A leather thong or rope attached to the skewer was then tied to a **sacred** pole. The men danced around the pole, blowing eagle bone whistles and pulling backward against the ropes until the skewers were torn from their flesh.

▼ A photograph of a Sun Dance gathering, taken around 1910. Even after many Plains Indians were forced to abandon traditional practices, many tribes still held annual Sun Dance rituals. The ceremony is still practiced on some **reservations**.

This self-torture was supposed to induce personal visions. The pain symbolized the sacrifices all members of society must make for the good of the group.

The Bear Dance

The Bear Dance was a Ute ritual that was eventually adopted by many other tribes. Every spring, after the first thunder of the season, the Ute would hold a Bear Dance to celebrate life after the long winter. During the ritual, people danced to the sound of rasps. A rasp is a notched stick that is rubbed or scraped with another stick to create sound. The sound of the rasp was meant to imitate the sound of a bear waking from its winter rest. In fact, the Ute word for a rasp is "bear growler."

A VISION OF VICTORY

In March 1876, during the conflict between the Lakota and the United States Army, Sitting Bull (right) led the Lakota, Cheyenne, and Arapaho in a Sun Dance. During the ritual, as Sitting Bull slashed his arms 100 times, he saw a vision of U.S. soldiers falling into the Lakota camp upside down, like grasshoppers dropping from the sky. The warriors took this as a sign that they would defeat the U.S. Army. The vision came true on June 25, 1876, when Sitting Bull, other chiefs, and their warriors defeated the Seventh Cavalry under George Armstrong Custer at the Battle of the Little Bighorn—which also came to be known as Custer's Last Stand. The Lakota called it the Battle of Greasy Grass Creek.

CELEBRATING THE DEAD

For Indians of the Plains and Great Basin, death was not something to be feared. It was accepted as part of the normal cycle of life. Everyone went to the same afterworld and continued to live much as they had on Earth, but without any problems.

Death on the Plains

There was not much mourning when an older person died. In fact, among some **tribes**, a sickly elderly person might leave the village to find a quiet spot in which to die alone. When a young person died, however, the people showed their grief in dramatic ways. The women cried and moaned loudly. In some tribes, relatives would cut off their hair as a sign of mourning. They might even cut off a body part, such as a finger or an ear, to show their grief. Comanche women wore rags when a loved one died, and they slashed their faces, arms, legs, and breasts.

Among most **nomadic** tribes, a dead person would be wrapped in a robe and placed high up on a platform or in the branches of a tree along with his or her possessions. The people would then hold a ceremony, with songs and speeches, to honor the deceased.

Some tribes buried their dead. The Wichita, for example, bathed the dead person and wrapped the body in a fresh bison hide. The body was then placed in a grave, which was covered with logs

◀ A photograph of an Oglala Sioux tree burial in 1880. The body lies horizontally in the limbs of the tree. The Oglala were one of many **bands** that practiced tree burials. Death was often accompanied by a ceremony to celebrate the life of the deceased. The ceremony might include singing and dancing, as well as stories about the person's life and accomplishments.

▲ *Dividing the Chief's Property*, a painting by American artist Joseph Henry Sharp (1859–1904), depicts the sharing of a Crow chief's property after his death. Sharp spent several winters in Montana living among the Crow, sketching their traditional customs.

and stones piled 4 feet (1.2 meters) high. The tribe buried some of the person's possessions with the body, and sometimes even killed horses and dogs to accompany their masters into the afterlife.

Death in the Basin

Among most Basin tribes, when someone died, the body was placed in the person's shelter along with his or her possessions. The house was then set on fire. People did not want to have contact with the person—or any of his or her things—after death. The rest of the band was also forbidden to use the dead person's name for a long time after he or she died. They believed that if the person's ghost heard his or her name, the ghost might come to live with the dead person's family.

The Northern Paiute wrapped their dead in blankets made of animal hides and buried them along with their belongings. The dead person's family members, who mourned for one year, cut off their hair and covered their faces with ashes to show their grief.

SOULS

The Assiniboine believed that every individual had four souls. When a person died, three of his or her souls also died, but the fourth remained alive. After the dead person's friends gave gifts to honor the deceased, this soul, which was now a spirit bundle, was released to the great spirit.

ROCK ART

Rock art—pictures painted or carved onto rocks—is one of the most ancient forms of human expression. Pictures that are painted onto rocks are called **pictograms**. Those that are pecked or carved into rock are called **petroglyphs**. For thousands of years, the Indians of the Plains and Great Basin created unique pieces of rock art.

Creating Art

Most petroglyphs were made by carving or pecking. An artist generally used a sharp rock as a knife to carve a design onto rock. To deepen the design, he carved the outline of the design over and over. To peck a design onto rock, an artist made a series of small pits in the rock surface. He probably struck a pointed stone with a heavier hammer stone to make these pits, or he struck the rock surface directly with his pointed stone. To make a line, he connected a series of pecked dots. Artists also used this pecking technique to fill in a drawing.

To create a pictogram, Indians used paints made from dried, ground minerals mixed with such oils as animal fat. The paint was often applied with brushes made from such plants as the **yucca**. Indian artists also used their fingers or pointed sticks as applicators. Sometimes the artist would simply draw directly on the rock with a lump of charcoal.

▲ Petroglyphs from Writing-on-Stone Provincial Park in Alberta, Canada, which contains the greatest concentration in North America of Plains Indian rock art. The petroglyphs and pictograms in the park were created by the Blackfoot Indians who lived in the area.

DATING THE ART

There are no scientific tests that can determine the age of rock art. However, the kind of drawing and subject matter can help establish a creation date for a particular piece of art. For example, early rock art often features such abstract designs as spirals and lines. Later art often includes hunters. The kinds of weapons the hunters carry (such as **atlatls** or bows and arrows, which came later) can help researchers determine an approximate age.

The greatest concentration of Great Plains petroglyphs can be found along the Milk River in Alberta, Canada, where they were carved into sandstone cliffs. Experts believe these artworks, which feature hunting and battle scenes, were made by the Blackfoot Indians. (Blackfoot is the name used by Blackfeet Indians living in Canada.)

The Coso Range in California contains the greatest concentration of petroglyphs in North America. Researchers have identified about 100,000 petroglyphs in the 91 square mile (236 square kilometer) area. These were created by such Great Basin **tribes** as the Shoshone. Many of the carvings in the area feature hunters and their prey—especially bighorn sheep. Experts believe, however, that this artwork probably had a ceremonial purpose. Basin Indians thought that the spirit of the sheep helped **medicine men** control the weather. In particular, it was believed that killing a bighorn sheep would bring rain. Researchers think that to bring rain, holy men created petroglyphs of the sheep instead of actually killing the animals.

▼ Shoshone petroglyphs carved in a rock wall in western Wyoming.

EVERYDAY ART

The Indians of the Plains and Great Basin incorporated art into their everyday lives. Plains people were famous for their elaborate **quillwork** and featherwork and the pictures they painted on **tipi** covers and bison robes. For the most part, Basin Indians' clothing and shelters were simple, but the women expressed their artistic natures with beautifully crafted baskets.

Adding Flair

Plains Indian women used porcupine quills to decorate clothing and other objects such as **cradleboards** and horse coverings. First, they cleaned the quills and colored them using dyes made from plants. They then attached the quills to the objects they wanted to decorate. After European contact, the women used beads as well as quills in their embroidery.

Featherwork was also an important craft among the Plains Indians. They used feathers to decorate everything from such **sacred** objects as pipes, **coup sticks**, and shields, to such everyday items as clothing and cradleboards. Perhaps the most famous feathered item used by the Plains

▼ A Sioux cradleboard shows the intricate beadwork that Indian women used to decorate everything from clothing to containers to horse coverings.

Indians was the war bonnet. This flowing headdress is one of the most recognizable symbols of the Plains Indians. Warriors wore the bonnet as a symbol of their accomplishments and honors.

Beautiful Baskets

Women living in the Great Basin made baskets from the many plants that grew in the region, such as wild rye. They decorated the containers by using different colored grasses and roots and by varying the weaving pattern. The baskets had everyday functions as collecting, storage, and cooking devices, but they were also used as ceremonial items in weddings and funerals.

THE WINTER COUNT

Plains and Basin Indians also painted beautiful designs on animal hides that functioned as diaries. The winter count (above) is a Shoshone tribal history painted on a bison robe. Each **pictogram** on the robe represented an important event from the history of the **tribe**. Every year the group would decide what was the most important event from that year. The keeper of the winter count would then paint it on the robe. Not only was the keeper in charge of the painting, he was also responsible for remembering what each symbol represented. In this way, the keeper acted as the group's historian. To ensure that this knowledge was never lost, each keeper had an apprentice. When the keeper died, his apprentice assumed his role and took on an apprentice of his own. This guaranteed that the history of the people would be passed from generation to generation.

COURTSHIP AND MARRIAGE

▲ A bird-shaped flute. Such instruments were used by Plains Indian men to woo potential wives.

On the Plains and in the Great Basin, marriages were often arranged by a person's parents. In many cases, though, the wishes of the young man and woman were taken into account, and matches were often made for love.

Finding a Partner

On the Plains, a young woman usually was allowed to select the man she wanted to marry. A young man, therefore, worked hard to win over the woman he desired. Often, a man would sit outside his beloved's **tipi** and play a special flute to woo her. The flute, which was usually made of cedar wood, was shaped like a bird's head with a long, open beak.

Before a young man's proposal could be accepted, he usually had to present gifts to the girl's family. After the Indians obtained horses, these animals became the most common bridal gift. Actual wedding ceremonies differed from one **tribe** to another, but most involved feasting, singing, and dancing.

Polygamy (*puh LIHG uh mee*), the practice of having more than one spouse at the same time, occasionally occurred in both **cultures.** Men or

THE TURNIP GAME

Cheyenne young people played an unusual courtship game. Groups of girls went out together to gather wild turnips and berries. As the girls returned to camp, they might find the path blocked by a group of young men. When this happened, the Indians played a game where the girls laid their turnips on the ground. The boys tried to steal the turnips, and the girls defended them by throwing sticks, dirt—even bison dung—at them. A girl showed she was interested in a boy by making it easy for him to take her turnips.

women usually took additional spouses only out of necessity. If a woman lost her husband, for example, the man's brother might marry her—even if he already had a wife. This provided protection for the woman, as well as a hunter to provide for her and her children. Sometimes if a woman had more work than she could handle, her husband might take another wife or wives to help out.

Hides were a source of wealth. Women prepared and dried the hides. Therefore, the more wives that a man had, the more hides that he could accumulate and use in trade with other groups. Likewise, if the number of men and women in an area was unequal, a man might have more than one wife or vice versa. Often, when a man had more than one wife, he married sisters. This reduced the likelihood of fighting among his wives, who all lived together in one lodge.

◀ A photo from around 1890 of an Apache bride wearing a traditional wedding outfit. Girls in Indian society were married much younger than women today. An Indian girl was considered ready for marriage usually by the time she was 13 years old.

Growing Up in Indian Society

Among Plains and Basin Indians, proper behavior was encouraged by example. Children were praised for a job well done. Unacceptable behavior in children was discouraged in the same way it was for adults—with the threat of ridicule and public humiliation.

Learning by Example

Until they could walk, Indian babies were strapped to **cradleboards** and carried on their mothers' backs. This arrangement allowed a woman to continue working while keeping her baby safe. In this way, the baby was introduced to everyday Indian life from the moment he or she was born. This was important, because Indian children learned their place in society by watching their elders.

▼ A Sioux family photographed in the early 1900's. In traditional Indian society, multiple generations of a family lived together. Parents, aunts and uncles, and grandparents all played an important role in a child's upbringing.

The Vision Quest

In Plains Indian society, the transition from childhood to adulthood was marked by a **ritual** known as the **vision quest**. A person discovered his or her guardian spirit during this ritual, which usually took place in his or her early teens. Although the specifics varied from **tribe** to tribe, most vision quests began with a ritual purification, such as bathing in a cold stream. The person would then go off alone into the woods, mountains, or another isolated place— and would go without food or sleep until he or she had a vision of his or her guardian spirit.

From the time a girl could walk, she accompanied her mother while she performed such chores as gathering wild foods and preparing hides. When boys were old enough, they learned how to hunt by watching the older men.

Indians usually lived in extended family groups, and many generations played a part in raising the children. Grandparents might amuse the children with traditional stories that served to teach the youngsters about the Indians' way of life. Grandparents and other relatives also helped discipline the children. When a young person showed desirable traits—such as honesty, bravery, generosity, and a hardworking nature—he or she received praise. If the child misbehaved, he or she was teased in front of the entire tribe. Indians did not believe in hitting their children.

All the tribes placed great emphasis on physical fitness. For people who lived off the land, being fit and active was crucial to their survival. The Indians of the Great Basin, who had to cover the greatest distances to find food and water, considered powerful legs of the utmost importance. As soon as a Paiute man heard his child's first cry, he ran far into the hills as fast as he could. The Indians believed that this would give the newborn the strong legs he or she would need to survive.

▲ A photograph from the 1870's of a Ute child and a baby in a cradleboard. Cradleboards were highly practical. They made it possible for a woman to keep her baby with her even while she worked. Soft padding on the inside made a cradleboard snug and comfortable, while the hide covering kept the baby safe from the elements.

SHELTER

The Indians of the Plains used different shelters than the Indians of the Great Basin. A group's lifestyle, needs, and available resources determined the kind of dwelling it used.

A Place to Call Home

The **nomadic** hunting **tribes** of the Plains lived in **tipis,** which could be set up and taken down quickly. The Lakota (Sioux) word *tipi* is a combination of the word *ti,* which means *to dwell* or *to live;* and *pi,* which means *they.* Among the Lakota, *tipi* literally means *they live.*

A tipi was made of long poles arranged in a circle and gathered together on top. The poles were covered with bison hides that had been sewn into one large covering. Early tipis were about 10 feet (3 meters) in diameter. It took from six to eight bison hides to make the cover. A tipi could be carried between camps by a dog pulling a device called a **travois.** After the Indians started using horses to transport their belongings in the 1600's, they were able to construct larger tipis—about 15 feet (4.5 meters) in diameter, covered by about 14 hides.

▼ A photograph of a Sioux camp taken some time after the 1860's. The Sioux and other Plains Indians usually situated their tipis so that the openings faced east to avoid the wind that generally blew from the west. The tipis also leaned slightly toward the east so that wind would flow over the top of the structure instead of pounding against the back.

▲ A reconstructed earth lodge at the On-a-Slant Indian Village at Fort Abraham Lincoln State Park in North Dakota. Mandan Indians lived in On-a-Slant from 1575 to 1781.

Indians on the prairie who raised crops, such as the Mandan, usually lived in **earth lodges** grouped around a plaza. The lodges were made of a framework of logs covered with willow branches, grass, and a layer of sod. Some groups made their lodges out of different materials. The Osage made rectangular dwellings out of mats or skins laid over a framework. These lodges measured from 30 to 100 feet (9 to 30 meters) long and up to 15 feet (4.5 meters) wide. The Wichita made grass lodges. These dwellings, which looked like beehives, were made of a circular framework covered by thick grass. The farmers also used tipis when they went on their annual bison hunts.

Basin Indians moved around so frequently that their lodgings had to be extremely portable. They often lived in **wickiups** (*WIHK ee uhpz*), which were simple structures made of a few poles covered with bark, reeds, or brush. In the winter, a layer of earth might be added to the covering for warmth. Sometimes these groups lived in caves near a reasonably plentiful supply of food and water. After they had horses, some Basin groups adopted the highly portable tipis because they traveled to the plains to hunt bison.

CLOTHING AND JEWELRY

For the Plains and Basin Indians, clothing was fairly simple. Most items of clothing were made of animal skins. However, these simple garments were often elaborately decorated with quills, fringes, feathers, and more.

Everyday Wear

Typical clothing among the Plains Indians consisted of a loincloth in the summer for a man. In the winter, he might wear leggings, a shirt, and moccasins made from animal skins. Women usually wore buckskin dresses. Any of these garments could be decorated with dyed porcupine quills, fur, fringes, and feathers. The bison robe was also an important piece of winter clothing for everyone in the **tribe.** The robe was made from the complete hide of a bison, including the hair. The hair side of the robe was worn against the body, and the outside was decorated with painted pictures.

▶ A Mandan bison robe from the mid-1800's. Designs were painted on the inside of the hide, with the fur side worn against the skin for warmth.

▶ A pair of Sioux moccasins made in the 1890's features the elaborate quillwork (top) and beadwork (edges) for which the tribe was famous. Bison heads, worked in quills, decorate the tops of the moccasins.

During hot weather, men in the Basin wore a loincloth made of animal skin. Women wore aprons that were made of animal skins or woven from bark. The Indians added leggings and fur robes or capes made of shredded bark during the colder months.

Not many Basin Indians had bison robes. They did, however, have warm robes made from rabbit skins. To make a large robe or blanket, a woman cut rabbit skins into long strips, which she then twisted into ropes. The ropes were then wrapped around cedar or **yucca** plant fibers and sewn together.

Headdresses

The Plains Indians' feathered headdresses were symbols of great honor worn only by men. They were made from the feathers of golden eagles, which were attached to a cap made of bison hide or deerskin. A band that went across the wearer's forehead was decorated with **quillwork** (later beads) and strips of fur that hung down on each side. Each black-tipped feather on a warrior's headdress represented a particular act of bravery.

HAIRSTYLES

Men on the plains often wore their long hair in braids, but many groups had very distinct hairstyles. Pawnee and Osage men shaved their heads, leaving a strip of hair in the middle. They often attached an **ornament** called a roach to the strip of hair. A roach was made of porcupine hair (not quills) or the tail hair from a deer, which was often dyed red. Feathers might also be attached to the roach. Men of the Kansa tribe plucked most of the hair from their heads, leaving only a small patch at the back.

BIG GAME HUNTING

The bison was the most important large game animal on the Plains, but the Indians also hunted deer and antelope. "Big" game in the Basin was not quite as large as on the Plains.

The Bison Hunt

For the **nomadic** Plains peoples, life depended on the bison, and even the prairie Indians who raised crops held annual hunts. Before they obtained horses, Plains Indians hunted bison on foot. A single hunter might cover himself in a wolfskin before sneaking up on a herd. Bison might run from a pack of wolves, but they would not consider a single wolf a threat. When the hunter got close enough, he would shoot a bison with a bow and arrow.

Communal hunts were held during the summer, when the entire **tribe** came together at one campsite. The people would wave robes or blankets to make a herd of buffalo stampede over a cliff or into a corral. They finished off the trapped animals with clubs, spears, or bows and arrows.

Horses made the hunt more efficient. After he shot one bison, a man on horseback could continue to chase the rest of the herd and possibly take down more animals. Shooting a bison from the back of a galloping horse required tremendous skill, however.

▲ A **pictogram** on a bison robe from the 1870's depicts a bison hunt. Hunting on horseback took incredible skill. A hunter had to race alongside his prey at top speed and, using a bow, shoot arrows while controlling the horse with his knees.

Big game was scarce in the Great Basin. The people in this area most commonly hunted jack rabbits, which they caught in large nets made from **yucca** fibers. Larger prey included mountain sheep and pronghorn antelope, which the Indians hunted using bows and arrows. Sometimes in the summer, groups of Indians gathered together for a communal antelope drive.

Preparing the Food

Many women accompanied the hunters so that the animal meat and hides could be properly preserved. The people ate their favorite parts of the animals, such as the bison tongue and liver, right away. They might even hold a feast to celebrate the successful hunt, at which freshly roasted meat would be served. The rest of the meat, however, had to be preserved for the journey home. The women cut the meat into thin strips and hung it to dry in the sun or over a fire. They also made a mixture called pemmican *(PEHM uh kuhn)*, which could last for months. Pemmican was made of dried meat that was pounded into a powder and mixed with bison fat. Occasionally, berries were added to the mixture for flavor.

WASTE NOT

Indians found a use for every part of the animals they killed. Experts have counted more than 85 uses for bison, in addition to using the meat and organs for food. Bison hides were used to make clothing, **tipi** covers, shields, and containers. The stomach and intestines were also washed out and used as containers. Bison bones were used to make tools and toys, including the runners for sleds. The animal's hair and sinews were used to make thread, rope, and the strings for bows. Even the animal's dung (often called buffalo chips) was used as fuel for the fire.

▼ An 1870 photograph of an Arapaho camp near Fort Dodge, Kansas, after a bison hunt. The Arapaho women have sliced the meat into thin strips and hung it up to dry to preserve it. Dried bison meat was a staple of the Plains Indians' traditional winter diet.

CAPTURING SMALL PREY

The Indians who lived in the Basin relied more on small game than on larger prey. In fact, these resourceful people even hunted rodents and insects to survive.

Water World

Archaeologists have found nets and hooks, indicating that Basin Indians sometimes fished in nearby streams and lakes. The men caught trout and silver shiners, and the women prepared the catch on the riverbanks. The fish were cleaned and cut using stone knives. Whatever was not eaten immediately was smoked, dried, and stored for winter.

In the spring, hunters also sought out the geese and waterfowl that **migrated** through the area. In Lovelock Cave, Nevada, archaeologists discovered duck decoys that are believed to be about 2,000 years old. They believe the Basin Indians used these decoys, made of tule *(TOO lee)* reeds covered with feathers, to attract their prey.

▶ Duck decoys, found in Lovelock Cave in Nevada, are believed to be 2,000 years old, two of the oldest known decoys in the world.

ANIMAL COMPANIONS

Basin Indians did not **domesticate** *(duh MEHS tuh kayt)* many animals. Archaeological finds show that they did keep dogs as pets, however. The remains of a domesticated dog, estimated to be more than 10,000 years old, were found at Agate Basin in Wyoming. Researchers can tell this dog was a pet because wild dogs have smaller jaws and bigger teeth than domesticated dogs. The Shoshone used their dogs to chase game. Some Basin groups also used these animals to carry their belongings when they traveled from camp to camp using a device called a **travois**.

Small Animals and Insects

Such small desert animals as ground squirrels, prairie dogs, lizards, rats, and gophers were important sources of protein for the Basin Indians. The Indians usually worked together to capture large groups of these animals in nets or traps.

Sometimes, in summertime, such insects as locusts, grasshoppers, and crickets swarmed into the Great Basin. The Indians dug trenches and beat the ground with sagebrush branches to chase the insects into the trenches. Once caught, grasshoppers could be roasted or boiled and eaten. They might also be ground up into a kind of flour and mixed with seeds and water to make a paste.

▶ A Plains Indian animal hide bow case and quiver for arrows.

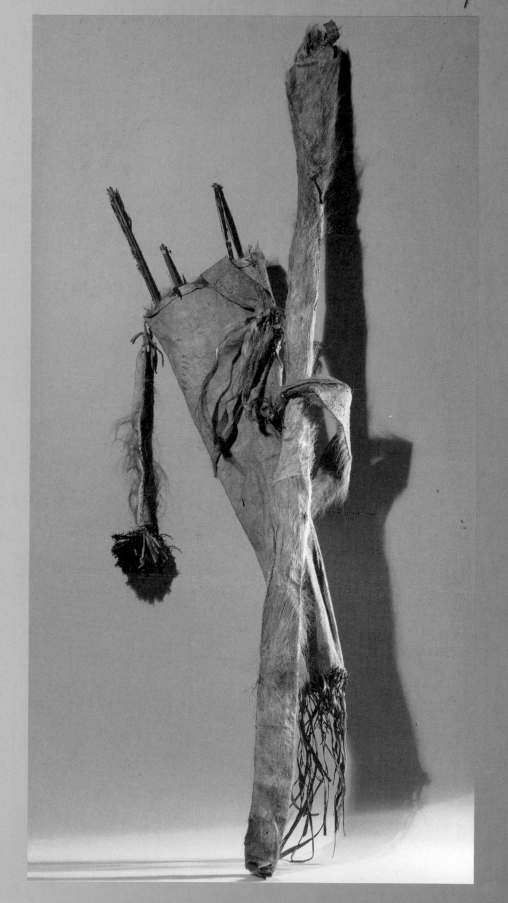

FOOD FROM THE LAND

Fruits, vegetables, roots, and nuts played a crucial role in Plains and Basin Indians' diets. For the Basin Indians, these gathered foods were more important to their survival than any game animals.

Harvesting a Meal

Farmer-hunters of the Plains, such as the Arikara, Kansa, Mandan, Osage, Pawnee, and Wichita, grew several crops, including corn. To plant their crops, the Indian women first turned the soil using a hoe or rake. The women then poked holes in the soil, using a sharpened digging stick, and dropped corn kernels into each hole. The farming **tribes** also grew pumpkins, beans, and squash.

After harvesting the crops, whatever was not eaten fresh was preserved and stored for the winter. Vegetables were usually dried in the sun. Corn could be dried on the cob or ground into flour. Squash was sliced into thin strips for drying. The people mostly stored their food in pits covered with grass, hides, and earth.

Gathering Nature's Bounty

The farmer-hunters supplemented their crops with wild foods. **Nomadic** Indians obtained most or all of their vegetable foods from the wild. Prairie turnips, plums, and chokecherries were commonly found on the plains, as were hazelnuts and walnuts.

◀ A woven Mandan basket from the mid-1800's, made of willow rods and bark with a leather handle. Such baskets were used by Mandan women to carry corn and other vegetables from their garden plots to the village. The position of the handle suggests that the basket was worn on the back, with the strap positioned around the forehead.

WATER WORKS

Most Basin Indians had to move around constantly in search of water. The Owens Valley Paiute, however, developed an **irrigation** system to survive in this **arid** region. Owens Valley, which is near Death Valley in California, has a stream that is fed by snows from the Sierra Nevada Mountains. Every year, the Indians built dams along the stream to direct the flow of water from the mountains to their valley. This irrigation system provided water for the people and the desert plants that grew wild in the area.

Basin women harvested cattails from the marshes. The insides of the shoots could be eaten raw or boiled. Once the heads of the cattails flowered, those too were boiled and eaten. Later in the season, when the cattail heads turned brown, the women gathered the pollen inside and made it into a cereal or bread. At this point, the plant's roots were collected as well. The roots could be roasted, steamed, or dried and ground into meal. Basin Indians also ate the roots of the **yucca** and other desert plants.

Seeds, including dropseed, wild barley, and ricegrass, were important food sources for the Basin Indians. The women added hot coals to a basket full of seeds and then shook the basket until the seeds were cooked. They then ground the seeds and made them into bread or a thick porridge. Acorns and piñon nuts were also staple foods. They were ground up and boiled to make a thin porridge.

▲ The Basin Indians used just about every part of the cattail plant for food. They also used its stems to make baskets and mats.

SPORTS AND GAMES

Everyday life was not easy for Indians of the Plains and Great Basin, yet they managed to find time for fun. Some games played by children were meant to sharpen the skills they would need as adults. Other were purely for fun.

Games of Skill

From the time they were little, Indian boys played at fighting or hunting. They were given miniature bows and arrows that they used to practice shooting at targets. Many **tribes** in North America played a game called hoop-and-pole. For this game, a large wooden hoop was made that was crisscrossed with rawhide straps. A player rolled the

◀ A 1900 photograph of a Sioux boy with a bow and arrow. Indian children were given the "tools of their trade" when they were very young. Boys practiced using their bows and arrows practically from the time they could walk.

hoop past a competitor, who attempted to stop the hoop by hitting it with a hurled pole.

Young men also sharpened their hunting and fighting skills with footraces and wrestling matches. Cheyenne boys started wrestling when they were about 8 years old. Competitors never used their feet or legs to trip an opponent. Instead, a boy's goal was to knock his opponent to the ground using only his upper body strength.

Just for Fun

The Indians enjoyed many ball games, including one similar to modern-day soccer. The Paiute played a game in which they kicked a buckskin-covered ball down a field, trying to cross the goal line of the opposing team.

Double ball, a game similar to **lacrosse** (luh KRAWS), was played only by women. Two teams competed to pass a pair of buckskin balls attached by an 18-inch (45-centimeter) thong across the opposing team's goal line. Using throwing sticks, the players threw the balls into the air and passed them to one another. The sticks, usually made of willow branches, were between 2 and 6 feet (0.6 and 2 meters) long with a kink at one end.

◀ A Sioux doll, made of buckskin and decorated with tiny beads. The doll's hairstyle, dress, **ornaments,** and moccasins skillfully reproduce actual Sioux clothing.

MAKING THEIR WAY

Travel was hard for the Indians of the Plains and Great Basin. For a long time, their main method of transportation was by foot. The acquisition of horses made life much easier.

Traveling on Land

Before they acquired horses, American Indians used dogs as beasts of burden. The dogs carried or dragged wood, meat, household belongings, even **tipis**. A small load might be strapped right onto the dog's back. Large dogs pulled a **travois**: two long poles tied together at the top to form an A-shape; and strips of rawhide lashed between the poles to form a carrying platform. The top of the travois was attached to the dog's shoulders, and the bottom dragged on the ground.

▲ *Blackfoot Women Moving Camp*, an etching by the American artist Edward Borein (1872–1945). Horses allowed Plains Indians to travel farther to find game and allowed entire **bands** of Indians to relocate quickly.

After Indians acquired horses, they used these larger animals to carry heavier loads. Hunters ranged farther to find food, and they could bring more meat back to the camp. This made it possible for more people to live together in individual camps. The Indians could also build larger tipis since the horses could drag a travois made of longer tipi poles, which could carry more household goods.

The introduction of horses completely transformed the lives of such Great Basin groups as the Shoshone and Ute. With horses, they could travel to the plains to hunt bison and would not have to rely solely on the meager provisions available in their home territories.

Traveling on Water

Basin Indians who lived near marshes or lakes used canoes to fish and hunt for water birds. To make the canoes, the Indians tied large bunches of tule reeds together with cattails. Two or three of these bundles were tied together to form a floating platform; smaller bundles were attached to create the sides.

Certain Plains tribes, such as the Mandan, used round boats called bullboats. The women made the bullboats by stretching a bison hide over a willow frame. The boats were used to carry loads across shallow rivers or streams.

▼ A photograph of a Sioux family and their dog, taken on a **reservation** in about 1890. Plains Indian dogs were an important part of tribal life. They were used as beasts of burden, as watchdogs, and for hunting.

SACRED DOG

Indians did not have a word for "horse." Different groups called horses different names after observing how the animal behaved and was used. Since many tribes used horses for tasks that had previously been performed by dogs, many names for the horse were based on the words for dog. For example, the Dakota called the horse sunka wakan (*SHOON kah WAH kahn*), which means *mysterious* (or *sacred*) *dog.* The Blackfeet called the horse ponokamita (*POH noh kah MIH tah*), which means *elk dog.* The Cree called the horse mistatim (*mihs TA tihm*), which means *big dog.*

MUSIC AND DANCE

Music and dance were important parts of American Indian life—and remain so today. To the Plains and Basin Indians, singing and dancing was the same as saying a prayer. They had special songs for all major events. Some songs were performed for public ceremonies; others to mark a rite of passage in an individual's life; yet others were sung while carrying out such ordinary tasks as setting up a **tipi** or hunting. Each had its own rhythm.

Making Music

Some Plains and Basin Indian songs had words, and others were strictly instrumental. The musical instruments they used included drums, bone whistles, rattles, and flutes. Drums were made by stretching an animal hide over a wooden frame. A two-headed drum was a large instrument that was hung from four wooden stakes. Several musicians played the drum at the same time using wooden sticks with leather tips. A hand drum was a smaller instrument that was played by one musician. The

▲ Men perform a traditional dance on the Wind River **Reservation** in Wyoming. Music and dancing continue to play an important part in American Indian **rituals** and ceremonies.

drummer held the instrument by a rawhide webbing at the back of the drum while he played.

Often, the rhythm of the drumming was different from the rhythm of the singing. The dancers followed the drumbeat, not the rhythm of the singers.

Some rattles were made from dried **gourds** filled with pebbles and attached to a handle. Others were made of animal hooves attached to a handle. Some rattles were made of rawhide sewn into the shape of a rattle head, then soaked in water and filled with sand. The hide stiffened into shape as it dried. The sand was then replaced by pebbles, and the rattle was attached to a handle.

GETTING IT RIGHT

It was very important that no mistakes were made when a person was singing a ceremonial song. The Indians believed that a mistake prevented the song from reaching the spirits. If that happened, the results could be disastrous. Much-needed rain might not come, or a hunt might be unsuccessful. To prevent mistakes, certain members of the **tribe** called prompters kept watch over the singers. If someone made a mistake, the prompter stopped the singing, and the singers started over from the beginning.

▲ A Plains Indian rattle made of rawhide. Decorated with an image of a bison, the rattle may have been used in hunting ceremonies.

THE BEGINNING OF THE END

Indians of the Plains and Great Basin were among the last **tribes** to suffer from the **encroachment** of settlers of European descent. From the mid-1800's on, however, their way of life changed steadily.

From Good to Bad

The first contact between Plains Indians and Europeans was made in the 1540's when the Spanish explorer Francisco Vásquez de Coronado *(frahn THEES koh BAHS kayth thay KOHR oh NAHTH oh)* entered Wichita territory (in present-day Kansas). Coronado, who considered the vast grasslands useless, left the area, and for the next 100 years, the Indians were left alone. By the late 1600's, French and English fur traders from Canada as well as Spanish traders from Mexico began passing through the northern plains and into the Great Basin. Many traded with the Indians in the area, and some even lived among them.

In 1803, after the United States purchased the Louisiana Territory from France, things changed for the worse. In 1804, the explorers Meriwether Lewis and William Clark set out to explore the country. Eventually, tales from the expedition encouraged other pioneers to head west. At first, they merely passed through Indian territory on their way to the Pacific Coast. Before long, the U.S. government built forts to protect the people who moved through the area.

▲ An 1868 photograph of a wagon train carrying supplies to workers building the Union Pacific Railroad. The construction of the railroad in the 1860's hastened the end of the Indians' traditional way of life. The new, easier way to travel encouraged many more people of European descent to settle on the plains.

SACAGAWEA

Meriwether Lewis and William Clark began their famous expedition to the Pacific on May 14, 1804. On November 4, Toussaint Charbonneau *(too SAN SHAHR boh noh)*, a French Canadian fur trapper who had lived with the Hidatsa, was hired as an interpreter. He was accompanied by his Shoshone wife, Sacagawea, the only woman on the expedition. Sacagawea was a tremendous help. She often provided food and medicine and was instrumental in keeping the men safe. Many Indians had never seen whites before. The presence of Sacagawea, and her role as an interpreter, made them accept the expedition as a friendly force.

The government signed treaties with the Indians, promising that the tribes would retain all rights to their lands if they would allow settlers to pass through peacefully. However, the discovery of copper, silver, gold, and other valuable minerals on Indian lands drew more people to the area. By the late 1800's, farmers were pushing onto the plains and claiming homesteads, even though doing so went against the terms of the treaties.

The building of a transcontinental railroad brought bison hunters into the area soon after the American Civil War (1861–1865). These men killed bison by the tens of thousands, merely taking the animals' hides and tongues and leaving the rest to rot. This drove the bison, the animal most important to the Indians' survival on the plains, to the brink of **extinction**. In 1700, there were more than 40 million bison on the plains. By 1895, there were fewer than 1,000 of the animals left. The destruction of the great bison herds increased hostilities between Plains Indians and the invading whites.

▼ An 1871 woodcut depicts hunters slaughtering bison from the newly completed transcontinental railroad. The government actively promoted bison hunting so that ranchers could raise cattle on the land; officials also wanted to weaken the Indian population as a way of keeping Indians passive. Railroads wanted the bison eliminated because the herds disrupted and damaged trains.

THE INDIAN WARS

By the late 1800's, relations between Indians and whites had greatly deteriorated. The Indians had been pushed off their traditional lands and moved onto **reservations**.

Fight for the Black Hills

In 1868, the Treaty of Fort Laramie guaranteed that the Black Hills territory in South Dakota would forever belong to the Indians, who considered the Black Hills a deeply **sacred** place. After gold was discovered in the hills, the United States government ordered the Indians to leave the area and to report to reservations. They were given a deadline of Jan. 31, 1876.

However, blizzards in January made it impossible for the Lakota Sioux to move across the land. In February, the War Department ordered the U.S. Army to go after two **bands** of Lakota Sioux—the Hunkpapa (led by Sitting Bull) and the Oglala (led by Crazy Horse). On March 17, the soldiers came upon a group of Northern Cheyenne and Oglala Sioux camped by the Powder River. This was not a war camp; only women, children, and elderly people were at the camp. The army killed everyone in the camp and burned it.

In June, Lieutenant Colonel George A. Custer was sent to round up those Hunkpapa and Oglala Indians who still had not reported to the reservations. He came to a village near the Little Bighorn River and, underestimating the Indian forces, attacked. At the end of the fighting, Custer and more than 260 other soldiers were dead. Sitting Bull and Crazy Horse had led their people to their greatest victory, but it would be their last. The final armed conflict of the Indian wars would be fought in 1890 at a place called Wounded Knee.

The Wounded Knee Massacre

Indians who moved to reservations could no longer roam the Plains and Great Basin to hunt or gather food. Reservation lands were often barren and difficult to farm, leaving the Indians to rely on the government for their basic needs. Unfortunately, these needs were rarely met.

▼ A Sioux painting of the Indian victory over the U.S. Army at the Battle of the Little Bighorn. Standing in the center are the Sioux chiefs Sitting Bull, Rain in the Face, Crazy Horse, and Kicking Bear—who made the watercolor painting.

▲ Sioux camp on the Pine Ridge Reservation, South Dakota, scene of the Wounded Knee Massacre. A government school building can be seen in the background.

THE DAWES ACT

The terrible living conditions on reservations finally caught the attention of reformers, who pushed the government for change. The government passed a series of laws, including the Dawes Act of 1887, which called for the reservations to be divided up into farms to be owned by individual Indians or families. However, much of the land was unsuitable for farming, and many Indians did not know how to farm. In addition, after land was given to Indians, all the "excess" land that was left over was auctioned off and sold to white settlers. Almost immediately, Indian nations lost huge chunks of their reservation land. Afterward, the Indians were encouraged to sell their individual holdings or lease them at far below market values. The Dawes Act's unintended consequence was, therefore, a massive loss of Indian lands.

The Indians' miserable living conditions gave rise to the Ghost Dance. A Paiute Indian named Wovoka *(woh VOH kuh)* said that if the people performed the Ghost Dance properly, the bison would return, non-Indians would leave the land, and the dead would come back to life. Although the dance was nonviolent, military leaders feared that large numbers of Sioux gathered together could overpower army troops.

On Dec. 28, 1890, about 350 Lakota Sioux sought by the army surrendered near Wounded Knee Creek in South Dakota. The band, about 120 men and 230 women and children, were followers of the Ghost Dance. About 470 troops surrounded them. As the troops disarmed the band the next day, someone—whether an Indian or a soldier is uncertain—fired a shot. The troops then fired on the Lakota. The Lakota warriors fought back but were greatly outgunned. Some experts estimate that up to 300 Lakota were killed. Twenty-five soldiers were killed. The massacre was the last armed conflict between the Sioux and the U.S. Army.

THE PEOPLE TODAY

For a time, it looked as if the traditional way of life of the Plains and Great Basin Indians would be lost forever. From the 1880's to 1934, the U.S. government actively sought to destroy native **cultures** by forcing the Indians to adopt an American lifestyle. The government seized Indian lands, outlawed traditional religions, and forced Indian children to attend boarding schools.

Since Indian children were educated away from their people, native customs and belief systems appeared to be dying away with tribal elders. However, the culture did not disappear completely.

Self-Determination

The Bureau of Indian Affairs is a government agency that once managed all aspects of Indian life on **reservations**. President Franklin Delano Roosevelt's Indian Reorganization Act of 1934 was intended to give Indians the right to govern themselves. This was not completely effective, though. Despite government promises, reservation Indians were allowed only limited self-government. The act did help put a stop to the destruction of Indian culture.

The Indian Self-Determination and Education Assistance Act of 1975, which Congress passed under pressure from American Indian **tribes,** put the tribes in charge of many of the decisions affecting their people. Among other things, this policy of self-determination allowed the tribes to increase their governing powers. Today, tribal culture is alive and well for many American Indian groups.

▲ A modern performer dressed in traditional ceremonial attire, which includes eagle feathers and a staff decorated with the head of a bald eagle. Because the bald eagle is an endangered species, it is generally illegal to own any part of the bird. The dancer is allowed to own these items because they have belonged to his family for generations. His eagle head, feathers, and claws are treasures registered with the U.S. government.

Traditional elements of Plains and Basin culture are again taught to Indian children, both on and off reservations. Such traditional crafts as **quillwork**, beading, and basketmaking flourish again. Native languages and traditional stories are taught to the children who one day will teach them to their own children. Underlying all of this is the importance placed on the cornerstones of the culture: a deep spirituality, strong family ties, and generosity.

Basin and Plains Indians are once again free to practice **rituals** and ceremonies that were once outlawed. Participating in gatherings called **powwows** is one way that Indian groups share their customs. At powwows, Indians from different tribes gather to sing and dance, tell stories, and share traditional foods and crafts.

Powwow

The word powwow originally referred to **medicine men** and other holy people. Today, the word is used to describe a tribal or inter-tribal gathering that includes singing, dancing, honor processions, traditional foods, and other expressions of Indian culture. Many tribes hold powwows to stay in touch with their history and culture.

▼ A Native American artist in South Dakota painting a blanket. Today, Native American artists continue to practice traditional crafts and try to maintain traditional Indian culture.

GLOSSARY

alliance A union formed by agreement, joining the interests of people or states.

archaeologist A scientist who studies the remains of past human **cultures**.

arid Dry.

artifact An object or the remains of an object, such as a tool, made by people in the past.

atlatl A spear-throwing device once used by many Indian groups.

band A group of several extended families, related by blood or marriage, that lived in an area.

calumet A **sacred** ceremonial pipe used by American Indians.

clan A group of people who are related through a common ancestor.

communal Something shared by a group.

coup stick A stick carried into battle by some American Indians with which the warrior tried to touch an opponent without killing him, as a mark of bravery.

cradleboard A small wooden frame to which an infant is strapped, usually carried on the backs of the women of most North American Indian tribes.

culture A society's arts, beliefs, customs, institutions, inventions, language, technology, and values.

descendant A child, grandchild, great-grandchild, and so on.

dialect A variation in a language used by a particular group of people.

domesticate To gain the ability to plant and grow specific crops, rather than simply gathering wild plants; or, to tame animals so they can be kept or raised.

earth lodge A dwelling used by some North American Indian tribes, consisting of a pit in the ground with the structure above it roofed with sod.

encroach To trespass upon the property or rights of another; intrude.

exile To send away from one's home or country, often by law as a punishment; banishment.

extinct Died out completely.

gender Sex, male or female.

gourd A vegetable that is closely related to the squash and pumpkin.

induce To bring on; cause.

irrigation Supplying land with water using ditches or other artificial means.

lacrosse A team sport played with a ball and sticks with net pockets.

matrilineal Tracing family relationships and ancestry through the mother's side.

medicine man An American Indian holy man, such as a priest or healer.

megafauna Large animals.

migrate To move from one place to another.

nomadic Moving from place to place in search of food.

ornament A decorative accessory.

Paleo-Indian A term for some of the earliest known human inhabitants of the Americas who lived from about 13,500 to 8,000 years ago.

patrilineal Tracing family relationships and ancestry through the father's side.

perishable Liable to spoil or decay.

petroglyph A rock carving, usually a picture or symbol.

pictogram A picture symbol in certain writing systems that could be used to stand for an idea, a sound, or a name.

polygamy The practice of having more than one spouse at a time.

powwow A festival at which many different tribes meet and that features such performers as storytellers, singers, and dancers.

quillwork Items decorated with porcupine quills.

reparation Giving compensation for wrong or injury done to another.

reservation An area of land set aside and reserved for American Indians.

ritual A solemn or important act or ceremony, often religious in nature.

sacred Holy.

taunt To ridicule, reproach, make fun of.

tipi A cone-shaped dwelling made of poles covered with hides.

travois A device consisting of two long poles harnessed to a horse or dog and trailing on the ground, used to transport possessions.

tribe A term that can mean a group made up of many **clans** that shared a territory and spoke a common language.

vision quest An initiation ceremony to help a person find his or her guardian spirit.

wickiup A dwelling built of poles and a covering of reeds, brush, or grasses.

yucca A plant found in dry, warm regions of North and Central America, having stiff, narrow, pointed leaves shaped like swords at its base and an upright cluster of white, bell-shaped flowers.

ADDITIONAL RESOURCES

Books

Daily Life in a Plains Indian Village, 1868
by Michael Bad Hand Terry (Clarion Books, 1999)

The Gale Encyclopedia of Native American Tribes, Volume 2: Great Basin, Southwest, Middle America
edited by Sharon Malinowski and others (Gale, 1998)

The Gale Encyclopedia of Native American Tribes, Volume 3: Arctic, Subarctic, Great Plains, Plateau
edited by Sharon Malinowski and others (Gale, 1998)

Native Tribes of the Great Basin and Plateau
by Michael Johnson and Duncan Clarke (World Almanac Library, 2004)

Native Tribes of the Plains and Prairie
by Michael Johnson (World Almanac Library, 2004)

People of the Great Basin
by Linda Thompson (Rourke Publishing, 2003)

Plains Indian Wars
by Sherry Marker (Facts on File, 2003)

Web Sites

http://americanhistory.si.edu/kids/buffalo/map.html

http://inkido.indiana.edu/w310work/romac/plains.html

http://www.mce.k12tn.net/indians/reports4/plains.htm

http://www.mnsu.edu/emuseum/cultural/northamerica/index.shtml

http://www.native-languages.org/kids.htm

http://www.pbs.org/lewisandclark/native/index.html

INDEX

Acknowledgments

Alamy: 10 (Craig Ellenwood); The Art Archive: 12, 20 (Gift of William E. Weiss/Buffalo Bill Historical Center, Cody, Wyoming), 16, 27, 35 (National Archives, Washington, D.C.), 23 (Bill Manns), 29 (Whitney Purchase Fund/Buffalo Bill Historical Center, Cody, Wyoming), 40, 46 (Chandler-Pohrt Collection, Gift of William E. Weiss/Buffalo Bill Historical Center, Cody, Wyoming), 50 (Gift of Corliss C. and Audrienne Moseley/Buffalo Bill Historical Center, Cody, Wyoming), 54 (Culver Pictures), 56 (Southwest Museum Pasadena/Laurie Platt Winfrey); Bridgeman Art Library: 11 (Museum of Fine Arts, Houston, Texas), 51 (Peter Newark American Pictures); Corbis: 4, 19, 33 (Marilyn Angel Wynn/Nativestock Pictures), 5, 59 (Layne Kennedy), 8 (Lowell Georgia), 13, 14, 28, 37, 38, 43, 55 (Bettmann), 31 (James L. Amos), 36, 48 (no photographer credited), 39 (Tom Bean), 44 (Smithsonian Institution), 52 (Swift/Vanuga Images), 58 (Lindsay Hebberd); Getty Images: 25 (Courtney Milne), 30 (National Geographic/Pete Ryan); Library of Congress: 26 (Edward S. Curtis), 57; Printroom, Inc.: 15; Shutterstock: 47 (Suzanne Tucker); Werner Forman Archive: 1, 41 (Chandler-Pohrt Collection/Buffalo Bill Historical Center, Cody, Wyoming), 9, 22 (no photographer credited), 17 (Utah Museum of Natural History), 18, 45 (The British Museum, London), 24 (L. Larom Collection/Buffalo Bill Historical Center, Cody, Wyoming), 32 (Museum fur Volkerkunde, Berlin), 34 (Museum of the American Indian, Heye Foundation, New York), 42 (H. W. Read Collection/Buffalo Bill Historical Center, Cody, Wyoming), 49 (Bradford Collection/Buffalo Bill Historical Center, Cody, Wyoming), 53 (Smithsonian Institution).

Cover image: Bridgeman Art Library (Private Collection)
Back cover image: Shutterstock (Joop Snijder, Jr.)